IDLING INTUITIONS: POEMS

IDLING INTUITIONS: POEMS

GUY CRAIG

THOUGHTS ON THE GOOD LIFE PRESS
Oregon, USA

IDLING INTUITIONS: POEMS

Published by

THOUGHTS ON THE GOOD LIFE PRESS

Portland, Oregon

www.ThoughtsOnTheGoodLife.com

© Copyright 2022 by GUY CRAIG

Poetry

Written by GUY CRAIG

Artwork by GUY CRAIG

Cover Design by SARAH CRAIG

First Edition

For inquires, write to the author, with the subject line "Inquires," at the email address below.

Hello@ThoughtsOnTheGoodLife.com

Visit - GuyCraigPoetry.com

This book is a work of fiction. Names, characters, places, and incidents either are the product of the author's imagination or are used fictitiously, and any resemblance to actual persons, living or dead, events, organizations, or locales is entirely coincidental.

ISBN: 978-1-7334968-4-1

For Sarah and Kenneth

SECTION I: HOME

Travel Without Touring   4
Family Ties   5
Propitiate Paths   6
Dreams   7
Walks   8
Provisioning   9
Produce You   10
Grass   11
Music   12
Arrived   13
Land   15
Home   16

SECTION II: TIME

Morning 21
Ways Once Lived 22
Sights 23
Sand to Stone 24
Dog Years 25
Traditions 26
Yard Games 27
Footprints 28
Tasks 29
Friends 30
Activities 31
Time 32
Afternoon 33
Tomorrow Gives Hope 34
Harvests 35
Chores 36
Listening 37
Family Gatherings 38
Returns 39
Fears 40
Futures 41
Tomorrow's Past 42
Unbound 43
Comparisons 44
Idle Space 45
Evening 46

SECTION III: IDEAS

Tolerance 49
Creations 50
Savings 51
Health 52
Loves 53
Reasons 54
Under the Weight 55
Forgiveness 56
Numbers 57
Living Free 58
Imposed Necessities 59
Patience 60

Notes 63
Acknowledgments 64

IDLING INTUITIONS: POEMS

SECTION I
HOME

Steps in all directions as confirmation

My mind as an engine—idling
Intuitions unpurposely deliver kinetic answers unknown.

—

Travel Without Touring

As the tractor shook, I thought:
"Engines at idle are still active."
The first answer that made sense
To me as to why there
Is not a more pronounced difference
In goodness between the curious young
Who travel and the curious young
Who stay home. Maybe elite private
Schools have the statistics on who
Improves most. I imagine it has
Less to do with where one
Goes and more to do with
Where one leaves. All things being
Equal, if it helps a youth
Thrive, travel seems the way forward
To a full and enriched odyssey
Of varied thoughts and telling tapestries.
Can my mind travel without touring?
I was the obligated and reverent
One who stayed. I needed more
Time to elevate what was before
Me. I care about other areas.
I'm old now, I rarely left
Home. I traveled through five generations
Of ancestors. I am them now.
Will future generations travel to me?

Family Ties

By name or blood, ties give
Until they break. Each generation learns
To journey between the sweet brightness
And the dimming colors of emotion
As the cost of fading connection—
The wealthy and powerful cannot always
Keep a temporal love of family
Against an untethered, immortal, free soul.
When the pain of banishment becomes
The only punishment to be applied,
Lost love grows with subtracted ends.

Propitiate Paths

I traveled to work by boat
On a tidal river. My dream
To not commute on the road
Sailed saliently with my day's satisfaction.
This was not just another trip
Of one memory. There I was—
A bit late—one more day
Dutifully making an effort to live
Like each day was my vacation.
On my way, to see anew,
I lightly floated with my ideas
On a wave to joyful writing.
Like finding an edit, I circled
Errantly to identify each river eddy,
Playfully watching for signs of others
Subverting expectations on propitiate paths home.

Dreams

How do you embrace a dream?
Often, I have kept openhearted within
The closed off world where retiring
Night chases hope around faintly found
Scents, feelings, sounds, colors, and light
Tears washed away with eye-pressed hands.
I infuse dreams in the land.
Every structure, person, animal, and plant
Line the perimeter of my purpose
To secure comfortable fields of contentment.

Walks

How many solutions have been secured
On a walk? Some people wish
To never walk away from problems.
The other day, in a dream,
I saw a problem walk away
From itself. It counted its numbered
Steps in all directions as confirmation
Of the inevitable end of intrusions.
It knew that some movements idle.
Culminations are created in the welcoming.
Answers to complex questions can arrive
While pondering leisurely thoughts that are
Asked casually on circular paths home.

Provisioning

I have always had a hunger
To provision for tomorrow's tough conversations.
A complete diet of ideas foster
Healthy outcomes on a growing body
Like a prepared pantry practically modulates
For hardships. Shortages often force local
Solutions to faraway supply chain cracks.
Ideas often have variable settled seasons
And each generation has tailored tables
To display the fusion of ingredients
From a world searching for cohesive
Confirmations that all the ledgers give
The same answer—we have enough.

Produce You

Outdoors or indoors, past or future,
Some long-held places inevitably produce you.
How else to fathom family land,
The gifts of generations in ties?

The land stores legacy and hope
In hidden improvements, margins, and maintenance—
Who has time for the past
Or the future when the present
Is a gentle and perfectly private
Summer breeze as you run free
And barefoot through the river fields
To the sandbar in the sun?

Grass

Grass is land's most expensive adornment.
A fragile fabric born of fire,
Floods, and consumed in empty fountains
Of famine, expressive of an unquenchable
Need to sanctify water not sand.
Farmed fields of grass seed tomorrow's
Harvests. Energy is stored as feed.
Grass has an expanding blue-skied soul.
Naturalists remember grass' perennially spiritual role.

Music

On stormy days, the steady drops
Of rain count in plant rhythms
Best heard and felt by being
Near the earth, trees, and flowers.
All the instruments of nature's home
Are like a local symphony playing
For the land and the sky,
Inviting and welcoming in cleansing soundscapes
Honored memorably by the soundly penitent-minded,
Gentle, imaginative, and the musically inclined.

Arrived

When you arrived—your new home—
How much did you make it
Like your old? Did you choose
A similar climate, with the summer
Wind? This land that almost held
You like when you were young,
Outside in nature, did you travel
Back to the beginning? I am
Your ancestor. I do not see
The fates, nor feel the fibers
As you possibly remember. I don't
Hear your homeland speaking to me
About how I might return someday.
All I taste is the air
I cannot breathe when I imagine
Not being here, where you saved
The family. I know love, loss,
And, a tie to this land.
Because of you, if I returned
Back to your homeland, I might
Not see how to live easily
Without the scent of Oregon myrtle
Trees, alder shade, and the harvested
Leaves used to season with summer
Flavors. I would miss the scents
In the river fields where flowing

Grass grows through sandy loam dirt
Ground deep below the old sea.
Some say to leave the home
I have known, should I believe
This land's peace will always follow
The generations who know the stories
And keep the subtle attachments maintained?
Given enough time, I am told,
The new wilderness becomes the old
Village. I say your daily prayer—
May all trails lead me home.

Land

"Old money" has bills to pay
On the lands of summer-flowered memories
And winter escapades in the snow.
They count privacy as the payment.
Property maintenance accounts are always emptied
First. As income declines, appreciation doesn't
Pay regularly like rents and crops.
With the land they live well
Enough to keep "old money" ways.

Home

A place to be more securely
Dry, where strong memories are stored
Gratefully on every newly granted gift.
Infused light with friendly fireside hopes
Warmly welcome acquaintances as honored guests.

The wealth of good fortune lives
Outside the owner and inside comfort
As a symphony of soulful celebration
And a lovingly solemn shared prayer
All in the same welcomed ways.

New wilderness becomes the old village.

—

SECTION II
TIME

Faced through ways once lived together

Morning

Dew waits on the morning leaves
To arrive timely to the soil
Where everything appears to be prepared.
Clear minds, mostly washed of weariness
From the day before, beckon light
To bend where a break will
Not do. Every morning leads ahead,
Even when the preceding night prevails
Against the idea of afternoon becomings.

Ways Once Lived

The prepared practice of heavy provisioning
Gains with the gathering of family
And friends who frequent the festivities
Each year and work to alleviate
The burdens of the communal body
And mind. Full shelves, now emptier,
Mark that close cousins are fewer
And farther away in new areas,
And friends are elsewhere now helping
Their own loved ones in need.
Memories bring forward the bittersweet understanding
That you may be the last
Remaining to remember the boisterous laughs
Escaped, voiced with past hurts lightly
Healed over with time and tenderly
Faced through ways once lived together.

Sights

The longer I live, the lovelier

I see the sights of seasons,

Experienced with erudite and earthy emotions,

Away from the arithmetic of attention

And the barker of bred banality.

Let the dawn have its due

Unencumbered from exigent views of etiquette

And free to flow where fair,

Ancient streams and starlight-setting shade sustains

Depth to delivered days and delightful,

Nestled nights. As the snow secures

The sun and showers, I savor

The weather with what time remains.

Sand to Stone

Ash poured in the river heals
Those who remain as a reminder
To return. Back to the beginning,
No longer altered by constant change,
The afternoon breeze washes the aridness
Through rustling filters of expanding fiddleheads
And fronds. The fonts and fountains
Of atonement slowly erode the commotions
Of conditioning from the long cadence
Of sagas turning sand to stone.

Dog Years

I sometimes count in dog years.
I add and subtract my pet's
Names with their number of years
Lived. Seven plus ten plus three
Equals the sum of our educations
Together. Each year, I am grateful
To measure those most meaningful friendships
In names spoken saunteringly to haunts.
As my mind faces the struggle
To remember my last sentences here,
Known names record my best account
Of joyful sounds and miles roamed.

Traditions

Stories settle on the evergreen leaves
This morning, intertwined with yesterday evening's
Moss threaded possibilities. Perpetual lessons press
Late afternoon-hued achievements. Every tomorrow spins
Spores of succession to secure traditions.

Yard Games

Yard games fly seasonally in flocks
To remind us that time spent
Away from good friends doesn't count.
Crowns for acuity and agility keep
The human mind and body buoyantly
In motion, tethered together as summer
Games enjoyably connected to fall realities
To better weather the wrought winter-hunger
Of early mornings and the madness
Of seasonally late, arrived, spring nights.

Footprints

I trekked hard today. I tread
The exact path twice. Like yesterday,
I watched my steps like words
Of a line. Each day written,
A couplet calls to remember economy
In starlight halls of December astronomy
Surrounded by an approximate isoverbal prosody.
My footprints were contained and light
On the earth this winter. Someday,
I may want to pursue paths
Far away again. Eventually, I might
Need to see the world's earth-toned,
Lightly-camouflaged secrets. I cannot clearly see
A reason to travel anywhere now.
Tomorrow, I will start traveling trustingly.
I'm now guided by generated words
Stored in electronic stations that consume
More water than all the reeds
Once cultivated to create the past's
Papyrus sheets. Scrolls are yesterday's internet
Signals seared. Printed books are solid
Reminders that some footprints should last.

Tasks

We toil to stay far ahead
Of where we will start tomorrow.
Each agenda is an ant farm
Filled with constrained possibilities by creatures
Unaware of the edges in life.
Lines in the earth measure progress
Often swept away in the sand.
Habit retrenches many finely carved paths
With newfound names. Old, repeated tasks
Mark our most worthy actual accomplishments.

Friends

The best of friends are limited
Goods in a world in need
Of people who feel like home.
A place can create an abundance
Of leisurely launches for long-traveled friendships.
Just the other day, we gathered
Where we annually return to laugh
The laughs of echoes in time.
Older, deeper, more broken and repaired—
Laughs carried every loving word forever
Spoken—a dialogue recorded for humble
Silence too. Like our friendship, gracefully
Granted as our particular good fortune.

Activities

Right back where it all started,
Yesterday is the goal for tomorrow.
There is a dizzying circular logic
In staying active to maintain slumbered
Joys and awakened actions to give
Each day a momentum in purpose.

From morning chores to calendared plantings,
We reactivate the tasks of life.
Obligations move with our spinning fears,
And only compulsion provides a glimpse
Of what must genuinely make us
Who we are in the activities.

Time

Time measures the expansion of loss.
Initial singularity gains space with time.
On the first day, joy was
Counted. Happiness is a thread tied
With oval-shaped, overlapping movements. Newly discovered
Worlds make mortality the first question.

Afternoon

Afternoon, for me, is summer first,
Spring starts before the fall leaves
For winter. I warmly sit fireside.
Which way do I go today?
On given gatherings, maybe a gin,
Green-olive infused martini nifter at four.
I can follow the leaves to
The sun or I can turn
In as they do for sleep.

Tomorrow Gives Hope

There is a place that lives
Off the present. A place exists
In probabilities and dreams explored beyond
The locked gates life may lead.

Tomorrow is a trail to follow
With time as a testament. Reason
Opens the paths to prepared opportunities
Ready for action. Tomorrow gives hope.

Harvests

Harvested crops bring together the seeds
Of shared knowledge as a store
Of planning to support greater abundance.
The prepared keep open a method
Of channeling chance in a place
Of their understanding to produce better
Harvests each year. The shared gift
Of cooperating with nature and community
Is a reminder to be hopeful
Those gains can be shared within
Time with generations who have felt
Happiest when they have been generous
With others, forgiving of themselves thoughtfully,
And hardily ready to work together
With open ways to bend, yet
Not break when the crops fail.

Chores

Not all work is created equal.
House chores are often given shelter
In the moral wrappings of holiness.
The idea of meditation is clean
Like the sanitary areas maintained by
Others who know they are still
Climbing to a position of choice.
Compulsions, chores, and choices are three
Ideas fit to work together to
Keep body, home, and community healthy
In the routines of thoughtful testament
And the tasks for thankful tomorrows.

Listening

Understanding is sometimes received by revelation
To tell us time is limited
In a world set to scale
With infinite possibilities. Chance seems unintelligible
In full vibration. Listening generates reasons
To live more humbly each day.

Family Gatherings

When lucky, long circuitous paths provide
Rich provisioned joys, surrounded most fully
By hearty laughs and light acts
Of leisurely perfection, as classic as
Canvas paintings rich with images recorded
In sweet sights made for tomorrows.

Returns

Surprise returns home are filled over
With the love of every unused,
Lost, buried, once reliably open trail,
Path, road, and route forever unknown.

High and dry when summer breezed,
Low and wet when most needed,
Moving home is open to yesterday's
Gains, present hopes, and future goods.

Fears

The falling leaf does not fear
The ground. It becomes an answer.
Only the sentient question the many
Ways to be happy and foster
Ever-increasing probable outcomes to better share
With others to produce more capable
Receivers of shared experiences. The courageous
Hold together, tightly wound to better
Represent a new place and time.
Filled with life and the opportunity
To be honored like the first
Mover. A home spins to hold
Life in an ark until known.

Futures

What comes after is the possible
Explanation for what came before all
Other present moments. Existence is theorized
And considered with multiple stringlike connections.

What consequences follow actions and decay
When all present bonds get cut
And hope frays by the fateful
Appearance of increasingly diffused core convictions?

Tomorrow's Past

We do not always know how
Others will name the world. Open
Hearts can hope to be strong
Enough to endure others who claim
They were gifted a bold vision
Full of words not everyone sees.
We can work hard to overcome
Tested techniques of disputation and decay.
Love is not needed to tolerate
Others. Sharing our wonder of life
We can together build tomorrow's past.

Unbound

Ideas find expression in the interlude
From conception to the awareness confirmed
That some of life is without
Simple answers. Consciousness is a creation
Celebrated when you realize nothing ends
In the way you once believed
It would. Allow for the space
To discover the desired and unexpectedness
Of life on the sometimes circular
Path of becoming. Enjoy the beneficent
Outcomes of patient wonder in knowing—
Meaningfulness is not bound to time.

Comparisons

I like to take a step

Far back from the increasingly varied

Choices before me. I make better

Decisions at just the right angle

In time and space. I find

Equations to test my future assumptions.

Comparisons create opportunities for eternal moments.

Contextualized vacuums of varied ideas concieve

Ways to better understand relative value

And foster objective ways to live

Better each day in the world

Around me. My clearest comparisons create

Measured judgments of society's past minds.

Idle Space

The known universe became expanding existence
In the idle space after time
Sequenced the inevitable paths to future
Destinations. All the answers ever shown
Lightly outline the world in opulent
Silence. We are still seeking answers
To questions waiting to be known.

Evening

Depending on progress and good fortune,
With family around me, I might
Be writing the stories both learned
And discovered through my own style.
To start work, I think deeply
About the Pacific Northwest rural river
Valley of my childhood. Would poet
Richard Hugo like my "triggering town?"
The place informs what I have
Found to be my life's subject:
Managing old family stories. Loving home
Enhances sweet feelings toward generous ancestors
And hides the fear of being
The one who loses the way
Without good reason. Even compassionate communication
To my emotionally invested loved ones
May not take away the sting
Of a shared legacy that will
No longer keep the family connected
And focused on a place shaped
By forward-thinking relatives of past dawns.

SECTION III
IDEAS

Peace, rest, and joy in promise

Tolerance

Love is not the only law
Capable of helping people more humanely
Live well together. History has shown,
Good neighbors do not always love
Time together. Sometimes we must yell
No. Even when preferring to whisper
Yes. We hope for complete concensus.
The views we hold can change
Over our lifetimes. We may reverse
Opinions we have securely held reverantly
Through the many years of tradition.
Tolerance is an idea that arrives
After we understand that even unbalanced
Conversation is concretely preferable to conforming
Our beliefs with others' new definitions
Of belonging. Even more equitable words
Born of a thoughtful, universal design
Can be misapplied injuriously when stolen
From the tested. When new thoughts
Are modeled to replace warm reason
With cold, measured, demonstrated-differences, only power
Changes direction. An hourglass isn't new
When it is flipped over. Filtered
Sand of the same size and shade
Is a tale of the trenches.

Creations

Sand dune shores near ocean waves
Whisper of the rise and fall
Of life. Catastrophic weather brings change.
Births swell, and deaths foretell fragily
Constructed existences only the sentient bemoan.
Space keeps sterile reminders of math's
Precision to rediscover every location known.
A loss heals when knowledge strengthens
The comforting conversations of meanings shown.

Savings

Keep some money if you can.
If you like magic, money illuminates
Wishes. Magicians are business titans, governments,
And banks. Money is electric now
To better flow around to protect
The unnatural wealth of extended health.
The wealth we trade to spark
The fire of shared survival through
The purpose dreams grant for comfort.

Health

Health is a root system. Below
Appearances are the specters of unknowns.
Feeling good is best understood heartily
Influenced by the deep belief in
Sleep as the mother of cures.

Loves

Silent and lost loves' sighs rhyme.

Heart pangs mark moments to remember.

First hugs, hands held, hopes hymned

Sail our dreams above the dell

To the place where we feel

No one has loved so sincerely,

Lost so innocently, and experienced completely

What a thousand granted consecutive lives

Could ever divine, decipher, or devise.

Reasons

The stars are the night's gift
As a compelling reason to count.
The precursor to the written word,
The daily questions and answers illuminate
An expressive world of received nature.

Seasons are the first epic poems.
Winds whisper the names of heroes
And villains. The first armies copied
Wild animals who battled in fields.
People are the satellites of land.

Under the Weight

From an open fire, the scales
Of justice measure unlimited goods without
Mass. Cryptic values shift with light
Ash underfoot. Many maligned, memorized mantras
Mark the young seekers of power.
Dry tear ducts of imagination crumble
Under the weight of burned books.

Forgiveness

Humbleness starts in the found awareness
That some answers will always stay
Lost to us. Parents understand children
Are born with an inexplicable essence
Of wonder. Children show the unfolding
Nature of wisdom. Peace gives insight
To help avoid hate and anger.
When grasping ways bend the world,
The weight of inexperience is measured.
Youths' hurtful words and actions hammer
With an emotional lightness when confronted
By the mature and grace loving.

Numbers

Utterances mechanically recorded with clay-calked hands
And twigs (the young's first swords)
Were born of fatigue and pain
With the stinging revelation that welts
Last longer in the dried mud
As a way to remember rations.
Margins created a desire for majesty
In the comfort of acquired trades,
Local treasures, and the verifiability provided
In trusted scribes. Numbers are priests.
Recorded marks are human's latest sacrifice
To a universe with signs unnumbered.

Living Free

Confined to the nature of incomplete
Knowledge of our own unfulfilled capacity,
Most need room for the option
To embrace the change that becomes
A constant. The forced will not
Abide long to live another way
When they have the knowledge before
Them of living free other days.

Imposed Necessities

Leisure studies seek good habits beyond
Life's minor diversions of imposed necessities.
Work is most often a coupled-capacity
Plotted in peaks and valleys. Time
Expands and contracts to the task.

Patience

Waiting is another name for time.
Patience was the first idea after
Creation. All ideas can be wholly
Discovered in the mind that knows
Spirit is a mixture of earth
And what is grown. Life becomes
Wrapped in a shell to protect
What may be before a response
And ahead of what comes after.
The spring sets to share summer
Peace, joy, and rest in promise
That everything is as it should
Be. Persevering life is not meager
In any meaningful and measured way.

Be. Persevering life is not meager

—

Notes

Idling Intutions: Poems uses the form "wordcount" as a "loose metrical structure" as elucidated by Lewis Turco in *"The New Book of Forms: A Handbook of Poetics"* (University Press of New England: Hanover and London, 1986).

"Evening": references Richard Hugo *(1923-1982)* the author of *"The Triggering Town: Lectures and Essays on Poetry and Writing"* (W. W. Norton & Company, Inc., 1979).

Acknowledgments

Thank you (to my lovely wife), Sarah Craig, who is immensely talented and a key supporter of my writing journey these last few years. She is the author of *The Holiday Window Painting Book*. Her MBA from Western Governors University and her Bachelor of Science in Journalism from the University of Oregon, original artwork, and publishing praxis through Thoughts on the Good Life Press made it possible for this third collection of poems to find its way out into the world.

Thank you, Michael McGriff, for recommending the works of Lewis Turco and Richard Hugo.

A warm and heartfelt thank you to my family and friends. Thanks for keeping me company on this journey. Your feedback and support continues to inspire me.

GUY CRAIG is from Coos Bay, Oregon, where he grew up along the South Fork Coos River. He lives in Tigard, Oregon, and he spends most of his free time in the Coos River Valley.

He holds a Master of Science in Special Education from the University of Oregon and a Bachelor of Science in Psychology from Portland State University. Guy is the author of three other poetry collections: *Coos River Reverberations: Poems of River, Farm & Forest (2021); Amble (2021);* and, *Mast Years: Poems (2022).*

Other Books by Thoughts on the Good Life Press

Coos River Reverberations:

Poems of River, Farm & Forest

By Guy Craig

Amble

By Guy Craig

Mast Years: Poems

By Guy Craig

The Holiday Window Painting Book:

How to Create Colorful Holiday Magic

By Sarah Craig

www.ingramcontent.com/pod-product-compliance
Lightning Source LLC
Chambersburg PA
CBHW060410080526
44583CB00012B/526